Heart Wisdom Process:
Understanding and healing the
subconscious

Paul Wong

Table of Contents

Preface

When I started my journey, I didn't plan on writing a book or creating this process. I was sick for a long time, and Western medicine wasn't working, so I went on a journey to look for answers. It started with alternative healing, which eventually led to the saints and ashrams of India over a ten-year period.

In this book, I want to share the great insights and observations from this journey, what I learned based on my healings and working with thousands of clients. The causes of life's challenges are found deep in the subconscious. Throughout the chapters, I will use the metaphor of "layers of an onion" when referring to the subconscious. Learning to work with the layers within the subconscious with the heart is the key to unlocking challenges and difficulties in relationships, physical health, finances, etc.

I will give you a framework based on my workshop teachings and private sessions, as well as the many questions I have been asked. This book is designed to give you a bigger perspective for understanding the source of your problems. You may need to read it several times to digest everything, and you may also need to use the process and techniques over a long period of time to get the full essence of this work. This is not a book to quickly read and forget. I hope you apply the book's techniques over at least a three-month period. If you can commit to applying what you've learned for two years, you will gain massive positive shifts in your life and undergo immeasurable personal transformation.

One key motivation for writing this book is to share what I've learned and help many people out there reduce their sufferings and solve their challenges. It is for both the novice and the advanced practitioner with decades of experiences. This is really a path for those with a deep passion for working on themselves.

This is not a traditional Western psychology book. It is more about the application of Eastern holistic approaches from China and India along with some Western methodology to transform sufferings. The techniques in the Heart Wisdom Process are simplified so that everybody can use them: beginners and even practitioners with professional practices.

Reading the book in sequence is recommended, as it is important to understand the individual chapters in order to grasp the bigger picture. If you don't follow the chapters in the order laid out, you might not be able to understand the ideas in later chapters, which are built on the ideas and techniques of earlier ones.

In first part of the book, I share insights about the nature of healing, the healing process, and its relationship to the Heart Wisdom Process.

Then, in the following chapters, I share information about the deeper roots of the causes of your life challenges. So, when you have a clear understanding of those roots, you can see what part of your life you've been unconscious of. Most of the deeper roots of pain are held in the subconscious, and that's why it's important to have knowledge about the subconscious and its relationship to the ego.

After having enough information and a framework of the causes of suffering, you can start practicing and applying the Heart Wisdom process.

I want to express my heartfelt gratitude to the sages in my life, teachers such as Amma Karunamayi, Hugging Amma, Ramana Maharshi, and others, for their support and knowledge on this journey.

I would particularly like to thank my partner, Sevinc Chelebi, who spent hours helping me put this book together. Actually, it was through her inspiration that I wrote this book, finally getting it done so that the teachings within can be available to many people.

Chapter 1

Introduction

I would best describe myself as a student of life and a big fan of self-help, self-development, self-discovery, self-realization, and anything to improve the journey of the Self. I can still remember listening to cassette tapes for programming the subconscious mind in grade school and high school and then to newly popular Tony Robbins about modeling human excellence using NLP. After college in late 1990s, I got trained in NLP and hypnosis and noticed that these techniques can help make people make significant personal shifts, getting rid fears and phobias and into high emotional states. These experiences fueled my desires to be some type of executive consultant or life coach, hoping to help others make positive changes to their lives.

It was not until 2006, when I got sick, that I started looking again for such answers. My sickness led me on a journey to find alternative ways of healing, one in which I traveled around the world. I spent a small fortune on numerous training and healing sessions from top teachers of both

Eastern and Western practices. With each session, my chronic conditions got incrementally better.

As I was healing, I discovered that applying alternative healing techniques and working with intuition was easy and natural for me. Repeatedly at trainings, other practitioners with many years of experience would tell me they were struggling to apply the basic teachings and connect with their intuition, while I rarely got mentally stuck. I seemed to just absorb and learn the teachings by osmosis, energetically, while others were mentally frustrated trying to learn intuition and healing with their left brain instead of just trusting that they were getting the right information downloaded from universal intelligence. This struggle is especially true for very left-brained people, and my programs are designed to help such people get connected to the right brain and feelings by working through subconscious blocks. When blocks are released, these people learn to trust their intuition deeply, and learning becomes very easy.

After receiving feedback from others, and because alternative practices seemed so natural and easy for me, I started a professional consulting and training business called Chinese Energetics. Clients from around world would find me on YouTube, where I have numerous demos giving tips on how to quickly relieve various physical pains and other life issues ranging from fears, phobias, anxiety, worries, etc. This resulted in invitations to teach seminars around the world.

Part 1
Nature of Healing and the Heart
Wisdom Process

Chapter 2

What is the Heart Wisdom Process?

Heart Wisdom Process

1. Awareness and knowledge of suffering, subconscious, and ego
2. Self-inquiry
3. Intuitive testing
4. Working with nine types of suffering
5. Personal transformation in the initial six-month period or two-year mastery period

Self-Inquiry

HWP applies the question "Who am I?" along with other specific questions to allow you to let go of the conditioning held in your subconscious.

Nine types of suffering

We identified nine layers of suffering in the human condition that are found in the subconscious. Working through and letting go of them can resolve most life challenges.

Intuitive Testing

Learn to apply intuitive testing related to the nine layers of subconscious conditioning.

Personal Experience of Releasing Layers

You must work through your layers of conditioning, experiencing and releasing them, to gain personal insight into your own subconscious.

Chapter 3

Beginning of the Heart Wisdom Process

Opening the Heart with Amma

Fast forwarding, I worked directly with probably a few thousand clients via sessions, workshops, and trade shows. Often times, I would get the feedback from clients that my work was very good but my heart was closed. Those comments hurt, and I could not figure out why they were saying that.

In 2012, the answer started to come, and perhaps it was a prelude of the Heart Wisdom Process. I received a blessing in the form of a hug from a humanitarian called Amma, also known as the "hugging saint." Each year, she gives millions of hugs to people to help bless them and relieve their suffering. She is known as a modern-day saint and incarnation of the divine mother, like Jesus's mother Mary, Our Lady of Guadalupe, Quan Ying, etc. After this initial hug, my relationships and perspectives started to shift significantly.

This led me to attend more programs and retreats with Amma. During one retreat, I spoke to a volunteer from her ashram. She was a sanyasi, which means a person who is renouncing living in the modern world and whose life is spent in an ashram in self- less service, meditation, yoga, and other practices for enlightenment. I asked her, "Why are you not wearing white?" Her response was "Amma asked volunteers to wear colors and normal clothes so newcomers don't see us a cult, which might make their hearts close." This message really sank in deeply, and I started to reflect on my own life. "What areas of my life are my heart closed to?"

This was the beginning of a journey of reflecting about all the people with whom I'd crossed paths– the people I didn't get along with and felt hurt, betrayed, and rejected by, the people and situations that I was angry about and that I'd wanted to avoid or protect myself from. I started sitting in meditation and opened myself to unprocessed feelings of heaviness, anger, and other uncomfortable emotions. That summer, and for months after, I sat and reflected, really connecting to my heart and being present to hurt feelings, and then the tears came forth. This was only the beginning for unraveling the layers of the onion. In Chapter 8, I will talk more about the significance of these saints and of working with the subconscious.

This self-reflection and opening of the heart was just beginning of the Heart Wisdom Process.

Complete Exercise for Opening the Heart

1. Ask yourself: "What areas of life are my heart closed to?"

_____

_____

_____

_____

2. Look at the list of people who have hurt and betrayed you and pay attention to your feelings. Ask yourself, "When I see them, do I want to avoid them? Do I have uncomfortable feelings that come up? Do I need to protect myself?" If the answer is yes, you have unprocessed feelings to work through.

_____

_____

_____

_____

3. While sitting, play movies in your mind of past experiences with these people. As you experience the events again, notice if you have uncomfortable feelings. If you do, then you have some work to do.

_____

_____

_____

_____

4. Later, after you have read the other chapters, come back to this exercise and apply the HWP to those past experiences.

_____

_____

_____

_____

Chapter 4

What is the Problem?

You can think of the unprocessed conditioning and programming as "trash" held as layers of subtle energy in the subconscious. When we don't take out the "trash," the garbage rots and causes all kind of problems in health, relationships, finances, unhappiness, etc. The problem is that most people have never been educated to take out the "trash" from mind and body until they have a major crisis in the form of physical illness, divorce, loss of a loved one, or some other immensely painful experience. Today's society puts significant value on the intellect and mind but does not emphasize connecting to your intuitive feelings and living from the heart. Due to suffering, people have been conditioned to avoid and suppress their feelings instead of learning to process them through the heart. This means that we need to connect to all of our feelings and learn to become vulnerable to fully experience emotions instead of pushing them down into the subconscious. We have been conditioned for a long time to avoid and suppress feelings to maintain a certain image, so learning to live differently, training yourself to process feelings through the heart, will take time.

The deepest unprocessed conditioning is related to previous life experiences connected to childhood or the suffering of parents that is passed on to the descendent. The life experiences are still held as "feelings" related to trauma, grief, anger, or other sorrows, and are connected to forgotten memories. All these experiences contain unprocessed energy held in the body, or "trash." These unprocessed sorrows will drain the body and make it highly inefficient. When you have subconscious memories of life that have not been processed, you will have downstream symptoms such physical pain, negative beliefs about the world, or even low energy. You have low energy because the subconscious deep roots are draining all your energy.

The accumulation of suppressed energies in the subconscious will eventually cause the mind-body-spirit system to break down. You can think of a new computer with new RAM and hard drive versus a used computer filled with unnecessary files never deleted. Eventually, unnecessary programs will overload the memory, causing inefficiency, and eventually the computer will crash. The same thing happens in life with the mind-body-spirit system. The breakdowns of life are failures in relationships, chronic health issues, loss of finances, etc. These are downstream effects of unresolved experiences in the subconscious.

If you don't resolve those experiences, then life will tend to repeat itself until you learn those lessons, as show in the flow diagram below. You may continue to repeat mistakes in business, attract the same types of relationships, and continue to experience physical suffering until you process the deeper subconscious issues.

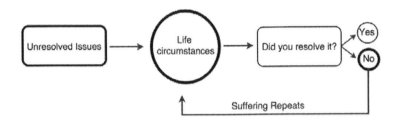

What Are the "Layers of the Onion"?

The "layers of the onion" really refers to the experiences of life that become layers of the subconscious or layers of the human ego. Even before birth, your subconscious mind and body are absorbing every single life experience and continuously adding to the layers. You are absorbing the experiences from the environment that you are born into, which includes all the influences and programming of parents, ancestors, family, friends, the collective, society, and others. These experiences form your stories, beliefs, attitudes, and behaviors that dictate how you respond to life. These experiences are held in mind or ego and are held in the body as subtle energy: "layers of the onion."

Regarding the layers, the surface layer is downstream of the river, while deepest layer is upstream. If you can work on upstream causes of suffering, then the downstream issues and symptoms will be addressed on a more permanent basis. HWP works by starting on downstream symptoms or effects and efficiently rolling back the layers until we get to the deepest issues. Sometimes the deepest roots can be so unconscious that the body and ego have been avoiding the pain and suffering for a long time. Because of the fear of suffering, they just won't go there until enough of the downstream issues are addressed.

HWP has the capacity to address both upstream and downstream together, relieving downstream symptoms while working through upstream causes.

Layers of the onion

Adult	Surface Layers	**9 types of suffering:** anger, sadness, grief, worry, fear, not safe, not loved, not trusting, not in control.
Childhood	Medium Layers	**9 types of suffering:** anger, sadness, grief, worry, fear, not safe, not loved, not trusting, not in control.
Infancy	Deep Layers	**9 types of suffering:** anger, sadness, grief, worry, fear, not safe, not loved, not trusting, not in control.
Prebirth	Deepest Layers	**9 types of suffering:** anger, sadness, grief, worry, fear, not safe, not loved, not trusting, not in control.

Chapter 5

What Is the Solution?

The answer is simple –take out "trash"!

We connect to subconscious feelings and release the layers through the energetic heart, the most powerful neutralizing organ for processing and dumping out the "trash." To solve the problems, we need get to the insights held in the deepest layers.

From working with thousands of clients, I observed that there are nine most common types of "trash." To take out the "trash," you communicate to the subconscious with simple self-inquiry. This self-inquiry applying an Eastern healing framework is called the Heart Wisdom Process.

We actually take out the surface layer of "trash" first. Then we can get the middle layers and eventually the deepest layers. This is how it works with subconscious. The ego especially, if it has incurred a lot of suffering, will not go to the deepest layers immediately because it is not safe. Often times, we must first work with the hurt ego of the adult, and when it feels safe enough, then we work with child's hurt feelings. Sometimes we have deep experiences of suffering going way back to before birth, to infancy, and to early childhood that are related to experiences of not being taken cared, of being abused, etc.

The surface layers consist of physical symptoms and momentary judgments, emotional responses, and general beliefs about life. But the medium layers maybe surrounded by recent experiences of life that have not been processed, such as those related to recent experiences of heartbreak and disappointment with current life relationships.

The deepest layers can often be connected to pre-birth and early childhood experiences. Inner-child work often deals with the deepest primordial fears, need for safety, or series of life experiences. As you peel back the layers that are deep enough, you start to deal with your relationship to existence and the meaning of life.

Chapter 6

Aim of the Heart Wisdom Process

The aim of this book is to help you become aware of the causes behind your life challenges, roots of suffering, and to give you a process for working with your subconscious and deepen your journey of introspection.

For practitioners, I encourage you to apply the practices on yourself first before applying them on clients. Being able to go deep within your own subconscious will give you deep insights for helping others. Each and every day, I continue to apply this process, and I find deeper understanding about life. If you don't do the work on yourself, you will not know the potential of this process and your own heart. Initially, after between one to three months, you will open a lot of doors to the subconscious, and it may be uncomfortable because hidden emotions, beliefs, and other long-buried issues that have been unconscious will become conscious. It is a detoxing period and can be difficult.

The much bigger, long-term aim is to train adults to develop awareness of their hearts, connect to intuition, and process subconscious feelings instead of suppressing and avoiding. This was the normal way of living in ancient times, but modern society has lost perspective, and people are now living out of balance with nature. For most people, it will take between six months and up to two years of regularly applying these practices to their lives because the modern world has conditioned many to maintain a strong and powerful image instead of being vulnerable and dealing with pain hidden in their subconscious. In a later chapter, I talk about "triggers," and if you have adopted the way of living put forth in this book and develop the awareness to work through your triggers, you will find the answers to the problems that block you from good health, success, and happiness.

Who is this for?

The Heart Wisdom Process can be applied universally by anyone looking for help with these areas:

- Health
- Relationships
- Wealth
- Career and Purpose
- Performance
- Personal Happiness
- Spiritual Growth
- Professional and Healing Skills

This work is for everyone who loves self-development. It is for novices looking for immediate help and those who have been on the journey for decades. It is also designed for beginners and for advanced practitioners looking to continuously development their life skills and to help their clients. No matter what skill level you are, you can find infinite ways to get better at your craft. I was an advanced practitioner for a number of years, but I still had to work through a number of unconscious blocks, and then my life and professional skills improved exponentially.

In short, this book is for someone:

- Who is looking for an answer for their repeating life challenges.
- Who is interested in self-healing.
- Who is interested in Eastern healing modalities.
- Who wants to support others, both friends and family.
- Who is a therapist, consultant, coach, doctor, or alternative practitioner.

Chapter 7

What Is This Book Going to Accomplish?

My aim is to share my practices with people who want to learn a new way of living life, who want to process their feelings instead of avoiding or suppressing them with different external experiences.

I encourage you to learn the steps, practicing the exercises of the book, in order to have a clear understanding about the process. This book was created to help you bring your subconscious patterns up to the conscious and let them go by using the steps I put together, which I call the Heart Wisdom Process.

With this book, you will:

- Develop awareness to understand the causes of suffering.
- Practice simple and powerful techniques to let them go.
- Practice intuitive testing.
- Work with the nine common types of suffering:

- Work with five types of suffering by applying knowledge from traditional Chinese medicine.

- Work with four types of suffering by applying knowledge of chakras from yoga teachings.

Chapter 8

Differences Between the Heart Wisdom
Process and Other Self-help Programs

Many self-help and other healing techniques are centered around offering immediate relief to feel better for many surface- level symptoms. We live in a modern society that does not value patience, and we are conditioned to be in an "instant" culture for everything, without getting to deeper causes. My Chinese Energetics courses teach my best techniques learned from multiple healing systems that offer immediate pain, stress, and emotional relief. Although they are still highly effective for relieving suffering, they have a limit. If you hit a limit with your techniques, then you need to look deeper.

HWP is a framework and process for letting go and releasing. It is a subtraction experience, subtracting layers from the ego, while others are addition experiences, adding layers to the ego. You will be losing layers of ego in the form of stories, beliefs, emotions, attachments, aversions, reactions, etc.

Other self-help and healing methods are well intentioned, but many are adding affirmations, new beliefs, coping mechanisms, strategies, or even adding energy into the subconscious. If you have not taken out the "trash" and you add more on top of old suffering, then the subconscious becomes more cluttered and confused. For example, if there is a deep wound from childhood and if you do affirmations or work to change beliefs by telling yourself, "I am powerful... confident...successful," what usually happens is that you might feel good and get an emotional high temporarily, but those good feelings wear out because old trash is still draining you. Many self-help methods distract people's minds from actually dealing with the subconscious, instead making people focus on something else to avoid processing suppressed negative feelings that need to be processed through the heart and neutralized.

The difference between the Heart Wisdom Process and other self-help processes or techniques is that it is mainly focused on "delayering" the ego rather than adding to it. Delayering means releasing the layers of subconscious energies with the heart instead of adding energies via more stories, techniques, affirmations, etc.

Many self-help methods involve mental strategies and coping mechanisms. Lots of them are done under what they call in the mind level, shifting of belief.

So, you can mentally shift the belief or use an affirmation, but if you don't get to the energy behind the belief, behind your story of life, and if you don't process through the heart, then the original source of the wound, of hurt feelings or sorrows, never gets processed.

Other techniques can make you temporarily feel better because your mind is distracting itself. But the source of suffering, the energy that creates negative beliefs in your mind, never gets released. You have to get to the source of the suffering.

Chapter 9

Background of the Heart Wisdom Process

For the last four years, I have been spending time in India with saints like Hugging Amma and Amma Karunamayi. When you spend time with the saints or holy people, teachers like that, they actually hold a very high spiritual vibration. Their spiritual energy is very strong. When in the presence of these people, who have been meditating for years and are highly self-realized, their spiritual energies actually help you to bring up the deeper subconscious patterns and let them go.

When spending time with these teachers, their spiritual energies bring up a lot of subconscious conditionings that you forgot about it. These conditionings are like different layers of the onion and explain why you are the way you are. Being in the presence of such teachers, spending time with them, brings lots of subconscious patterns up to the surface. Sometimes it is possible to experience pain before you let these patterns go. This is the nature of healing. First, you bring all conditionings up and then let them go. During this period, you can experience emotional or physical detoxing.

The self-inquiry process discussed in the technique chapters was developed through chanting the Gayatri Mantra. Usually, at ashrams, the gurus would give students a japa mantra practice. It serves the purpose of activating spiritual energies and reducing the thoughts in the mind. Those who have devoted significant time to the mantra practices can receive personal, worldly, and spiritual benefits. It was after reading Amma Karunamayi's book, *The Secrets of Gayatri Mantra Revealed*, that I took on this practice. From repetitively chanting this mantra for few years, the insights of self-healing and processing subconscious conditioning were revealed or downloaded to me.

It was the combination of a series of key lessons learned from the darshans of Hugging Amma, mantra teaching and meditation practices of Amma Karunamayi, and jnana yoga teaching of Ramana Maharshi, plus Instruction from Eastern and Western teachers and my personal healing journey that contributed to the development of the Heart Wisdom Process.

Chapter 10

Nature of the Healing

We are born with specific parents, family members, nationality, culture, and collective and social influences around us. Based on their experiences, beliefs, habits, behaviors, life skills, and ways of living, we are conditioned to be who we think we are. If we are born and raised into an environment with more positive attributes and to parents with good beliefs, qualities, habits, life skills, etc., we are likely to be conditioned in the subconscious to have positive and similar responses.

If we are born and raised into a negative environment, our subconscious is programmed with negativity and less-desirable attributes. If the environment in which we grow up has more love, patience, and compassion, our subconscious is programmed to see the world with these perspectives. If the environment is more competitive, violent, or abusive, our subconscious may see ourselves as not lovable and not deserving, and the world as threatening and unsafe, and there will be a constant need to protect ourselves.

Most humans have mixed bag of positive and negative programming in the subconscious, making up their personalities, who they are and how they react and respond to the world. This doesn't mean that people born into abusive and adverse environments don't overcome their challenges.

Some of my clients are very successful professionally. They are physically attractive. Some are company owners and executives earning high incomes. They have nice homes and beautiful spouses but are constantly seeking happiness from outside. Although they have achieved a high degree of success and have everything from a wealth standpoint, they are still unhappy on the inside. They are highly stressed and burned out with work, suffering in relationships, and hold resentment toward loved ones. If their subconscious experiences are not resolved, these successful individuals will often experience self-sabotage. They experience losing external accomplishment through divorce, financial loss, and physical issues. If you track their journey through life, they had suffering early on and then started to work harder. Then they produced wealth and much material success. If they did not have earlier sufferings but their ancestors' experiences were passed down, then their subconscious will contain the energy of their sufferings, and that must be released. However much they have achieved, the source of suffering in the subconscious has not been resolved. For example, maybe the subconscious still contains experiences of not feeling loved, not being accepted by their father, or the fact that they grew up in a poor environment, looked down on by others for not having wealth. Other examples include being unattractive at a young age and now looking physically beautiful, but they feel unhappy and see themselves as ugly. Often times, if the subconscious experiences are not resolved, these people will experience self-sabotage, and even though they have achieved much, they end up losing external accomplishments through divorce, financial loss, and physical issues.

Exercise

1. List areas of life you are successful yet feeling stressed and unhappy.

_____

_____

_____

_____

2. Write down any growing up experiences that motivated you to become successful.

_____

_____

_____

_____

3. Write down any programming or conditioning from parents, ancestors, and others that have influenced you to be successful.

_____

_____

_____

_____

4. After reading the later chapters, apply the HWP to the experiences that created triggers. Write down your experiences.

_____

_____

_____

_____

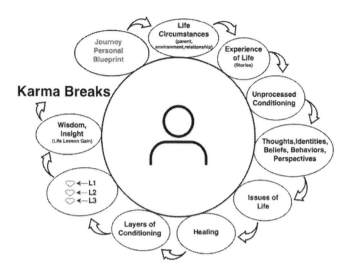

If you look at the diagram, the environment creates experiences of life, which are our stories. These experience "stories" are then stored in the subconscious. The story of past experience is held in the subconscious mind and the energy from the experience is held in the body. That's why when you tune into memory and observe yourself, you can feel some kind of feeling connected to an experience even if it already happened. When you go through your life experiences, you will have more and more stories and energies connected to those stories. They start to build up in the subconscious mind as unprocessed conditioning. The conditioning or experiences, good or bad, will create further thoughts and will form your perspectives, identities, and personalities of who you think you are.

More deeply ingrained experiences from childhood will start from your surface-level beliefs and judgments, which create your attitudes and behaviors. Your current life challenges/ issues are essentially the effect of the gestalt of all your life experiences, from the deepest rooted experiences, personalities, and identities to your current beliefs, behaviors, and attitudes.

The external environment will trigger unconscious responses. It may be the news of violence, abuse, a co-worker or partner getting angry, etc. Then the subconscious feelings of not being loved or not feeling safe get re-experienced. What happens in life is that most people are taught to cope instead of processing these unconscious responses through the heart. When they get processed through the heart, the energy connected to the feelings of earlier life experiences can get released. Then it is no longer held in the subconscious mind as a story.

When the layers of stories are processed and released through the heart, then usually clients will experience insights about life. They will experience more love and be compassionate for themselves and the people that hurt them, and sometimes they feel a greater sense of oneness and connection with universe. These are some possible insights. When they gain these insights, repeated experiences of suffering often cease because they have learned the lessons of life.

Part 2

Sources of Life Challenges

Chapter 11

What Are the Sources of Programming/Conditioning?

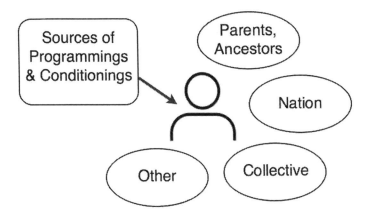

The subconscious mind gathers all experiences and holds them in the body from birth to your current age. Good or bad experiences located in the subconscious mind are also held in the body.

1. The good and bad experiences of parents and multiple generations of ancestors can be passed on to you and held in the subconscious and in the body.

2. Another group is the ethnicity and nationality that you are a part of. There are some countries or ethnicities that have suffered persecution over the centuries. These experiences are being passed on into the subconscious as well and held in the D.N.A. These are conditions that make you who you are.

3. The third group is your collective or the social groups and social environment that you are a part. By being around a certain group, you start to adopt those views, behaviors, and ways of being.

4. The last group would be other lifetimes. You have experiences from these lifetimes held in the subconscious. If you have experiences of suffering, or programming or teachings from other lifetimes, they are also part of you and held in the subconscious.

   In hypnosis, they use a technique that is called "past life regression." With this technique, you can regress, go to other times and dimensions, and connect to the experiences that caused you suffering.

Chapter 12

How Do We Get Programmed?

Conditioning is based on our life experiences, on the experiences we have growing up, and also comes from our parents, friends, family, the collective, the culture, and our nationality.

Stories - Conditionings create Ego

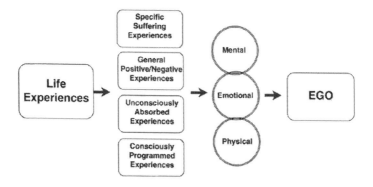

The diagram highlights that people are conditioned through four categories of programming. The first is a person's specific sufferings, either those from parents and ancestors or those associated with your environment. It can consist of physical suffering experienced through violence, abuse, war, or other trauma. It can be one's own emotional suffering related to grief, loss, anger, etc. Or it can be mental stress or abuse, or suffering caused by fighting and arguing.

The second category is made up of the general positive and negative experiences that create your identity and self-image. These are a lot of more deeply rooted attachments. For instance, you might have had the positive experience of somebody telling you how attractive you are, and then, later in life, somebody else says, "You're ugly" or "You're not attractive." Even though you have a positive self-image and your identity is one of being attractive or beautiful, when somebody says something that contradicts who you think you are, you get very upset. Another example would be when you have the expectation of yourself as a highly responsible person but don't actually live up to that expectation. By not meeting the self-image that you're trying to live up to for your family or for your friends, it can be very disappointing for you and can cause you suffering.

It is the same for negative identities or self-images. For example, take the person who used to be overweight but who has now taken care of their weight. Physically he/she is more attractive, but internally they don't feel attractive because they're still holding on to that self-image of being overweight and not attractive. The person is still not happy inside even though, on the outside, they look nice. Some people can be wealthy now, but still behave with survival responses and live in fear because they experienced poverty earlier in life. Now, even with more wealth, they are still living with old programs and behaviors, as those subconscious movies are still playing in the background.

The third category is related to unconsciously being conditioned. We absorb a lot of the beliefs, attitudes, and viewpoints of others by osmosis, especially when we are young. We absorb both positive and negative. If our parents are hardworking, then we will absorb that attitude, but they might also have anger or negative behaviors such as being aggressive or fighting, and we can absorb that too. Their attitudes, mannerisms, and behaviors are passed on to us unconsciously, and we adopt them as our way of being.

The last category is being consciously programmed. We can consciously program ourselves by routinely doing things and being repetitive. If you do something for ninety days, it becomes part of your routine, part of your habit.

So, these are the four ways in which we become conditioned. This conditioning creates our mental perceptions, attitudes, views, and judgments.

The Heart Wisdom Process is about working through all of these areas, especially the areas of suffering caused by negative mental beliefs, viewpoints, emotions, and reactions on the physical level. By working with all these areas, that's how we can reduce suffering.

Chapter 13

Understanding Programming and Conditioning

The difference between programming and conditioning is that programming is the input that goes into mind and body while conditioning is the effect of the input. Once the programming goes into your subconscious, it becomes a conditioned response. The input may cause you to react and create a series of other inputs and conditioned responses later.

Your movies, your "stories" of life, are your programming, and they condition you to form viewpoints, perspectives of life, and also your automatic behaviors or responses. Life is one long movie made of a series of movies and plots with a beginning and an end. If you have positive movies, you will experience pleasurable feelings and be conditioned to expect them again in the present or future. If you have bad movies, you will experience uncomfortable feelings or pain, and you will be conditioned to expect pain to occur again. Your experiences are the programming and conditioned responses stored as energy in the subconscious.

Immediately after you have an experience, you will be conscious of it because it is fresh in your mind. Over time, your conscious mind is likely to forget, but the subconscious mind still remembers, as the event is still happening because the energy behind the experience never got released. Then the movie of the event in the subconscious lies dormant until there is an external stimuli or trigger.

Repeated positive or negative life experiences will condition the mind and body to have either positive or negative expectations. The human mind and body is no different than Pavlov's dog being conditioned to salivate with the ringing of the bell. TV or radio commercials condition you by associating having lots of fun and being around attractive people with particular products. Then you subconsciously feel drawn to take action because the ego and subconscious want to experience pleasurable feelings. On the other hand, negative stories in the news associated with violence, death, and other suffering will also trigger pain. In each case, the pleasure and pain conditioning can cause problems in life. If the energy of pleasurable and painful conditioning is not released from the subconscious, then you can be easily manipulated or relive the pain over and over again.

The conditioned responses of your parents, family, and ancestors can be wired into your subconscious as well. Those energies can be passed on for generations. When you experience external stimuli, it can trigger pleasure or pain responses, and you can have a variety of automatic responses. Often times, people have no conscious awareness of why they say certain things or behave in certain ways. This conditioned response will continue to be in your subconscious until the energy behind it gets released.

The Heart Wisdom Process releases not only the energy behind your negative stories but also that of the positive stories. This means that the external experiences cannot manipulate you. If you have made the decision to improve your intuition or connect to your inner guidance, the conditioning of negative and also positive experiences must be released so that you can have clarity with your intuition.

Chapter 14

Understanding the Subconscious

Life is one long movie. It starts before birth and continues to your current age. Every movie is fully experienced by the conscious mind and body through the five senses. It is then recorded as a memory into the subconscious mind and body as a story and as physical sensations. Once the experience has past, your conscious mind will forget it, but the subconscious will still remember everything because energy in the subconscious is holding the story and body sensations.

If the energies behind your positive and negative experiences are not released, then negative or positive beliefs and expectations are formed about life. These beliefs will then dictate your attitudes, behaviors, and ways of life. You are likely to either directly experience suffering or experience the stories of suffering from parents and family, ancestors, collective social groups, and your culture and nationality. You may absorb beliefs and ways of life into your subconscious without even knowing. Whether consciously experiencing or unconsciously absorbing life, the accumulation of experiences in your subconscious creates the layers of the ego. All these layers of experiences, these "stories," are held together by energy.

The energy in the subconscious is connected to your feelings. You can do a simple exercise. Connect to a memory, either positive or negative. Imagine the experience again in your mind. As you replay that movie, you will notice body tension, tightness, contractions, and other feelings associated with the experience. If you still feel those feelings of the past experience, then the energies in the subconscious have not been released, and they won't be until they are processed through the heart.

If subconscious energies have not been fully released, the external world will continue to trigger you, whether through your boss, spouse, family, or others. These triggers, or hot buttons, will bring out emotions such as anger, disappointment, sadness, fear, grief, etc. Even though they seem like surface-level emotions, they are often connected to earlier periods of your life.

The early development period of life, from pre-birth to adolescence, is responsible for the most deeply rooted beliefs and emotions held in the subconscious. These feelings are responsible for how you deal with stress in the present day. Growing up with negative experiences in unstable, abusive, or volatile environments may train the subconscious to perceive the world as unsafe, threatening, and not loving. If your beliefs or suffering were passed to you from your parents, family, ancestors, and others during those developmental years, the subconscious will be impacted, and you are likely to operate with more fight or flight responses.

The programming and unprocessed experiences in the subconscious from your direct experiences, especially from the early years, and from your parents, ancestors, the collective, and society are the causes of suffering in your current life, whether in health, wealth, finances, or happiness.

Part 3
Understanding Suffering

Chapter 15

Programming Creates Ego

Below are the most common types of programming in the human condition. These are programs that go into the subconscious either through direct teachings or by being unconsciously absorbed. If you were not raised by parents, then it is the programming of the adults and influencers in the environment you grew up in.

- Parents' direct programming and teachings
- Parents' approval and disapproval
- Parents' expectations, ideals, and demands
- Parents' ways of being programmed and absorbed into the child's subconscious
  - Emotions – fears, worries, anger, sadness, grief
  - Issues related to safety, approval, trust, control
  - Judgments, criticisms
  - Self-image
  - Personalities, characteristics, mannerisms, etc.
  - Beliefs, perspectives

- o Stories of suffering
- o Attachments and aversions
- o Life skills – math, music, craft, etc.
- o Attitudes and behaviors
- o Positive and negative habits – ex: hardworking vs laziness
- o Person's direct or indirect experience of suffering (trauma, abuse, bullying, etc.) while growing up
- Person's experience at school with teachers, peers, and friends while growing up
- Person's experience with family members while growing up
- Ancestral programming
- Societal, cultural, ethnic, and national influences
- Media influences

The subconscious starts recording before birth and continues to the current age. The most vulnerable periods of life are pre-birth, infancy, childhood, and adolescence. The younger you are, the more vulnerable you are. Any suffering that occurs during these times will form the deepest-rooted subconscious beliefs and perspectives about life. Suffering during these times can be most harmful for development and can result in more severe problems later in life.

Here is a list of some of non-nurturing life experiences that can significantly impact a person's life:

- Abuse
- Violence
- Death
- War
- Trauma
- Drugs/alcoholism/addictions
- Divorce
- Poverty
- Bullying
- Fighting
- High competitiveness
- Conditional approval/disapproval
- Excess worry, fears, anger, grief
- Excess criticism/judgments

Conditioning from life experiences (programming) in the form of beliefs, attachments, aversions, identities, desires, coping strategies, and past emotions are wrapped in layers. The ego is a gestalt of all this conditioning, which is responsible for present- day self-image, attitudes, and behavioral responses.

This flow diagram below presents an overview of my understanding of the human ego and its relationship to suffering. Particularly during the early development period, from pre-birth to adolescence, good experiences and good feelings create attachments, and negative experiences create aversions. These experiences create our ego, the sense of "I," or who you are, essentially a gestalt of all your experiences that forms your personalities, self-image, identities, beliefs, perceptions, ideals, and expectations toward life. Based on past experiences, the ego will adopt strategies to seek good experiences (pleasure) and coping mechanisms to avoid suffering.

The ego keeps building layers and layers until there is enough suffering to have a physical or nonphysical breakdown in life. When this happens, some people will gain insights, learn their life lessons, and be able to turn their lives around. When they have experienced the "dark night of the soul" or a spiritual awakening, they are then drawn to self-help techniques focused on delayering the ego. They embark on an opposite journey – instead of building the ego, they are letting go and releasing layers from the ego.

You will be working with the list of programming above and will use the HWP process to delayer the programming and conditioning from your own past experiences. You will be working through the beliefs, attachments, aversions, identities, emotional responses, and behaviors you learned consciously and unconsciously from parents, ancestors, collective groups, nation, culture, and other influences. You will be likely to process through the issues related to non-nurturing periods of life as you work from the surface to the deepest layers. The deepest issues will be related to the child's experiences with safety, survival, love, and approval.

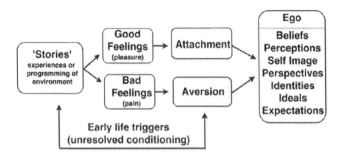

Exercise:

1. List your own experiences, from birth to the present day, related to suffering (Ex: trauma, divorce, violence, loss, death of somebody, abandonment, poverty, not feeling loved, not feeling nurtured, etc.).

_____

_____

_____

_____

62

2. Conclusions and beliefs about life after these experiences.

_____

_____

_____

_____

3. Life experiences while growing up related to mother, father, family, environment, culture.

_____

_____

_____

_____

4. Life experiences related to your personalities (identities).

_____

_____

_____

_____

Chapter 16

Ego and Coping Mechanisms

In the previous chapters, you learned how programming creates the ego and how the subconscious contains the unprocessed conditioning connected to our feelings. The everyday person in modern society has not been educated to see the connection between feelings of stress and subconscious conditioning dating back to pre-birth. People are not taught how to deal with and process their feelings. Instead, they are programmed for generations to use various coping mechanisms to distract and avoid feelings.

Coping mechanisms give temporary relief, but subconscious feelings never get processed and the energies behind them never get released. Then the cycle of sufferings and coping continues and repeats until a greater mind-body shutdown occurs.

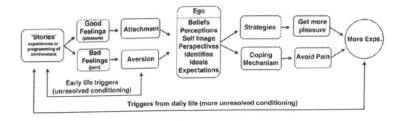

Some examples of coping mechanisms:

- Food

- Alcohol

- Drugs

- Shopping

- Video games

- Drugs

- Sex

- Exercise

- Positive affirmations

- Surfing the internet

- Busyness

- Workaholism

All these coping mechanisms can give a person temporary relief. Some coping mechanisms such as exercise and busyness can even give positive benefits like better health and productivity, but you may be unhappy and unsatisfied with life because the unconscious suffering has never been processed.

If you are using a favorite way to avoid dealing with feelings, sometimes the universe will create situations that take away your coping mechanism. For example, when an avid runner twists an ankle and can't run, she no longer can get the physical high from exercise, and instead, she has deal with her feelings during her recovery.

To better illustrate this point, when I attended silent meditation retreats, participants were required to disconnect from all aspects of life such as the internet their phones and remain in complete silence for seven days. You couldn't talk to anyone but had to be with yourself and your feelings. It was very difficult for many because many of the subconscious feelings they had been avoiding through distracting and coping mechanisms came to surface. It was highly uncomfortable for participants and many wanted to quit the silent retreat halfway through the program.

Some examples of subtle coping mechanisms:

- Smiling
- Being the center of attention
- Sarcasm
- Talkativeness
- Anger

- Criticism

- Being judgmental

- Pride

- Arrogance

The purpose of this book is to get people to reflect on themselves and why they are the way they are. You might have even subtler coping mechanisms you are unconscious of. If you do have automatic default behaviors, they provide a good opportunity to look at your programming and why you have been conditioned to be like this. Take time to reflect and apply the HWP to the experiences and programming that created these responses. They might be connected to early life experiences of not feeling loved, safe, protected, etc.

Exercise:

1. List your coping mechanisms (Ex: shopping, drinking, etc.).

_____

_____

_____

_____

2. Reflect and list experiences that created the need for these coping mechanisms.

_____

_____

_____

_____

3. List any subtle coping mechanisms you might have.

_____

_____

_____

_____

4. Reflect and list the experiences that created the subtle coping mechanisms.

_____

_____

_____

_____

5. After reading the later chapters, apply the HWP to the experiences that created these coping mechanisms. Write down your experiences.

_____

_____

_____

_____

Chapter 17

Unresolved Issues Cause Triggers

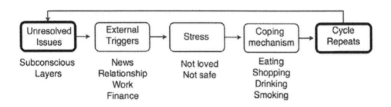

If we have not resolved conditioning held as energy in the subconscious, then the external world will "trigger" us to feel stress. These are the buttons that get pushed and are connected to conditioning in the subconscious. When these buttons are pushed, it triggers fight/flight reactions and negative emotions.

Generally, if you get to the root of almost any problem in life, it boils down to unprocessed experiences in the subconscious related to "not being loved" and/or "not being safe."

Examples of Triggers:

- Criticism of boss towards employees
- Suffering on the news related to abuse, violence, or types of injustice
- Arguments and judgments from a lover, close friends, family, etc.
- Getting insulted
- Cheating and dishonest behaviors
- Death or tragedy
- Loss of finances, worries about bills

Look at your own triggers in life and start reflecting. See if you can draw a connection between triggers and early life experiences. The same triggers now are likely to have been created or experienced in pre-birth, childhood, and adolescence.

Your own current triggers can be the same as those of parents, family, ancestors, and from your environment while growing up. If your parents or ancestors experienced injustice or suffering, then you can absorb similar beliefs and responses, both consciously and unconsciously.

Often, behind your triggers are the "shoulds" and "should nots" of life. These are rules you, your parents, or other key influencers took on over the years. When people experience suffering, they create rules to try to control life with the hope of eliminating repeated suffering in the future. When pain in the subconscious has not been resolved, the ego becomes highly attached to following rules, resulting in triggers and more suffering.

I remember how I used to be a very angry person because my mother was also an angry person. She despised and hated people who were dishonest and unethical. As I was dealing with people in business, I also tried to enforce these beliefs and rules. I was miserable and angry, and it took huge toll on me emotionally and physically.

This was actually a huge lesson as I spent a summer working on all the "should" and "should not" rules inside my head and connecting them to all the subconscious feelings related to my anger issues. In the beginning, I was not conscious that I had so many of her dysfunctional ways of life, which she had passed on to me even though she'd had good intentions of living honestly and ethically.

I would encourage you to start reflecting on all your triggers and your own rules and beliefs about life, especially those that have been passed on. Ask yourself the question: "Is this belief, emotional response, or behavior even mine? Or did I pick it up somewhere in life?"

Exercise:

1. List of triggers (Ex: boss, lover, co-worker, family, etc.).

_____

_____

_____

_____

2. Reflect and list any experiences that created triggers.

_____

_____

_____

_____

3. After reading the later chapters, apply the HWP to the experiences that created triggers. Write down your experiences.

_____

_____

_____

_____

Chapter 18

Conditional Love Creates Suffering

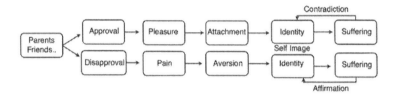

This flow diagram shows the cause and effect of conditional love and its relationship to suffering. When we are growing up and if we get approval and disapproval, the subconscious experiences good feelings and bad experiences and they are recorded in subconscious. Repeated approval conditioning such as compliments and praises create attachment to keep those good feelings while repeated disapproval such as judgments and criticisms create aversions.

The nature of the ego is that seeks pleasure and avoids pain. Suffering occurs when you become either attachment to positive feelings and aversions to negative feelings. Both aversions and attachments create identities that form our self-image.

If you have received approval for grades, looks, success with sports, you can identities, 'I am confident..., I am good looking..., I am smart.' Then, as years go by and you are no longer in high school anymore, you are not as good looking or popular as you once were, but you are likely to still reminiscing about the past and holding to those past identities. Now, in the present moment, someone may comment, criticizing your looks or judging your results, and if you are attached to the past, then you are likely to get upset and experience suffering.

Experiencing disapproval can create identities like "I am ugly," "I am weak," and "I am fat." These identities are formed as you experience life, and then they go into the subconscious. Those who formed identities due to criticism, judgements, or being made fun of at a young age, have low self-esteem and identities of pain.

Take, for example, kids who are overweight or unattractive when they are young and get bullied or made fun of so that they form identities based on the thoughts "I am weak, "I am ugly," and "I am fat." What happens next is that over the years, they workout, lose weight, and make themselves attractive. In the present day, however, even though they are attractive and successful, they are still unconsciously holding on to the unattractive self-image of the past.

Exercise:

1. List any experiences of conditional love (Ex: parents, friends, work).

_____

_____

_____

_____

2. List identities created from conditional love (Ex: ugly person, strong person, etc.).

_____

_____

_____

_____

3. After reading the later chapters, apply the HWP to experiences of conditional love. Write down your experiences.

_____

_____

_____

_____

Chapter 19

Expectations and Idealism Create Suffering

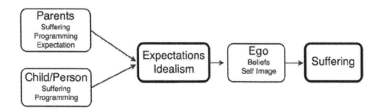

This diagram illustrates how expectations and idealism create suffering. This chapter further expands your understanding of triggers from Chapter 17. Becoming attached to expectations and ideals creates triggers and suffering. The sources are your life experiences, parents, ancestors, the collective, society, and culture.

When your parents and ancestors experienced suffering, they formed conclusions about life. Generally, parents desire to pass on what they've learned from their mistakes to the next generation so their children have better lives. This suffering in the parents' subconscious creates expectations of what life should and should not be. Then the kids become conditioned to meet these expectations of how life should be played out. If they meet expectations, they receive approval from their parents, and if not, they receive disapproval.

Your own life sufferings will also create expectations of how you want life to be played out. If you had really good parents, you may have created the expectation that you will attract someone like your parents. If you had abusive, narcissistic, or uncaring parents, you may have the expectation that you want a future partner who is the opposite of your parents. Here, again, your expectations are created based on attachments and aversions, as discussed previously.

Society, culture, and the media in the modern world also play a significant role in how expectations and ideals are created. The movie industry in the last century has created a lot of images of the perfect man and perfect woman, detailing how they fall in love and lively happily ever after. The problem is that expectations and idealism create suffering because they put intense amounts of pressure on people to fit their lives into a particular box according to their ideals about what "perfect" is.

Examples of these ideals are: "I will be married at this age," "I will have this kind career," "My spouse will look like this," and "I will retire at this age and live happy ever after." These ideals are formed by many people, especially young people, and when those ideals and the happy movie do not play out the way people want them to, those people experience suffering in their relationships.

If you want to reduce suffering, a key life lesson is to learn to accept life as "What Is" instead of opposing it, to accept life on its own terms rather than yours. Life will present a variety of situations, circumstances, and role players that are quite different than your expectations and ideals. If you oppose and fight with life, then you are going to be more miserable. This principle can be very difficult to follow because so much programming is not even conscious.

Initially, I worked on myself for hundreds of hours regarding "shoulds" and "should nots," but for some situations, it took months and sometimes years because my conditioning was so deep and unconscious.

Two every good contemporary spiritual teachers who teach accepting life as "What Is" are Byron Katie and Adyashanti. I remember how Adyashanti once spoke to a man whose son was born with a debilitating condition. In the man's mind, he had the perfect son movie planned and played out. His son was going to go to college, have kids and a family, and live happily ever after. He suffered for a long time because he never grieved and let go of this ideal life for his son.

Another similar example is that of an athlete reminiscing of the past and how, if he had not gotten injured, he would be a pro player living a different life than the one he has now. If you have any similar experiences or regrets, you must grieve and let go of the expectations for the life that "would have been" or "should have been." The energy connected to the grief held in the body must be let go.

Exercise:

1. Write down the areas of life where you are not happy regarding relationships, finances, health, or anything else.

_____

_____

_____

_____

2. Reflect and write down the expectations behind your issues.

_____

_____

_____

_____

3. Ask yourself where these expectations came from or what the experiences or sufferings were that created them.

_____

_____

_____

_____

4. Ask yourself what would happen if you let go of them, and notice your responses related to these attachments.

_____

_____

_____

_____

5. Ask yourself what would happen if you did not meet these expectations or ideals. Do you feel disappointment, resentment, or other emotions?

_____

_____

_____

_____

82

6. Find the "shoulds" and "should nots" behind expectations and let go of the energies through your heart.

_____

_____

_____

_____

7. Ask yourself if you are accepting life as "What Is" or if you are still opposing "What Is."

_____

_____

_____

_____

8. After reading the later chapters, apply the HWP for letting go of expectations and ideals.

_____

_____

_____

_____

Chapter 20

Suffering and the Ego's Long-term Strategies

The diagram below illustrates how the ego puts together a long- term development as a result of suffering and why, even though success has been achieved, a person can still be unhappy and experiencing life challenges.

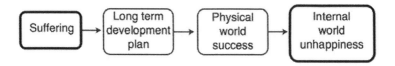

Suffering Example #1: Beaten up by Bullies

A boy gets beaten up. He is angry and helpless during the experience. He develops himself through martial arts and weightlifting. Now he is better able to protect himself. He is bigger and has more muscles. Internally, he still has anger and resentment toward the bullies. He feels pride and arrogance for overcoming his difficulties and carries a chip on his shoulder.

Suffering Example #2: Made Fun of and Unpopular

A girl is unpopular and made fun of at school. She develops herself over the years by losing weight and wearing nice clothes. She looks attractive and thin now. Internally, she still holds the self-image of the ugly kid from the past. She still doesn't feel good enough, worthy, or deserving of love.

Suffering Example #3: Poor Growing Up

A boy grows up in a poor environment. His parents are in constant fear of not being able to survive. He works hard over the years and makes a lot of money. Internally, he still worries, has fears, and is often stressed out about survival.

These are real examples of clients and successful people. They had suffering earlier in life that caused them to find long-term development strategies to solve the problem. Over the years, they did solve the problem physically, but internally, they are still suffering because the subconscious energies never got processed and released.

The question for you is: "Do you have success in the external world yet internally feel unhappy or feel something is still missing?"

Exercise:

1. List your long-term strategies.

_____

_____

_____

_____

2. List the experiences that created your long-term strategies.

_____

_____

_____

_____

3. After reading the later chapters, apply the HWP to the experiences that created these long-term strategies. Write down your experiences.

_____

_____

_____

_____

Chapter 21

Nine Types of Suffering

Now that you have a better understanding for the causes of suffering, we are going to have learn the techniques for dealing with it. Here are the nine layers of suffering associated with the Heart Wisdom Process. Over the years, I have worked with numerous clients, and regardless of life issues, these are the layers that seem to be most commonly repeated.

The art of this work is to be able to be intuitive and to communicate to the subconscious in the right sequence. It is no different than using a combination lock. If you enter the right password, the lock opens. If you communicate with the subconscious in the right order, then the issues get resolved.

Also, as you unravel the layers, deeper ones in the subconscious will become conscious and come to the surface. You must be patient on the journey because, depending on your situation, the ego might have lots of letting go to do before life improves.

The first five most common types of suffering come from the basics of traditional Chinese medicine:

1. Sadness – Heart
2. Grief – Lungs
3. Fear – Kidneys
4. Anger – Liver
5. Worry – Stomach

These are the basics of human emotions. We're going to be using this framework to identify the different layers that we're going to be working through with the Heart Wisdom process.

In TCM, the consciousness of each emotion is associated with a particular organ. Sadness is the natural consciousness associated with the heart, grief with the lungs, anger with the liver, fear with the kidneys, and worry with the stomach. Because of the imbalances of life and of modern society, people are no longer processing emotions and living according to the ways of nature as they did in ancient times. You may find emotions stuck in the body in a way that does not correspond to the natural order.

For example, as you are doing the HWP work, you may find sadness, anger, and grief in the stomach, and anger, fear, and worry in the heart area. You will have to use your intuition to detect the imbalances and communicate to the subconscious to release them.

The next four most common types of suffering come from the knowledge chakras of yoga.

6. Not safe

7. Not loved

8. Not in control

9. Not trusting

These four common types of suffering are found in almost all issues. Life experiences will have the energies of these components held in the subconscious mind and body. If you have had any experiences of not feeling loved and/or safe, then you have a wound on the inside. This will cause you to lose trust in life, whether of a particular person, situation, or the divine. The natural tendency of the ego is to not experience the suffering again, and you will find ways to control future life experiences in order not to experience the pain again.

The energy components of (1) not safe, (2) not loved, (3) not in control, and (4) not trusting are stored in the subconscious as layers. As we discussed in earlier chapters, non-nurturing experiences will have significant impact on these key issues.

As you work through these issues related to your present life challenges and as you peel back the layers, you will find the same issues occurred in your adolescence, then back in your childhood, and then possibly going back to infancy and pre-birth. You may not have direct experiences of suffering causing you to not feel safe or loved, but the programming of your environment might have passed these subconscious feelings into your being.

As you work with physical and nonphysical life issues, you will find yourself consistently applying and working with these nine types of suffering over and over again.

When I started my consulting and healing practice years ago, I did not see these patterns of suffering within the layers. Back then, I used the Chinese Energetics techniques and indeed helped people feel better, but I did not thoroughly work through the layers. Knowing about the nine types of suffering and how to work through layers can systematically produce results for you, especially for resolving deep wounds. This can give you profound ways for reducing suffering and increasing well-being in many areas of your life.

Part 4
Techniques

Chapter 22

Intuitive Training and Sensing of the Nine Types of Suffering

Below is a series of exercises for training you to sense the nine types of suffering connected to the layers. This will help you become aware of the body's responses and feelings. Learning to become aware of the body's feelings associated with an experience's "story" is important for learning to communicate with your subconscious.

You will go through each of the nine types and experience the feelings associated with the experiences. You will learn the commonalities of how your body reacts to the feelings associated with each of the nine types of suffering within the layer. Then you will compare and contrast them to understand and feel the differences.

You may close your eyes or keep them open while doing this, whichever is easier for you to sense those feelings connected to the experience. These exercises are designed to help train your intuition so that as you are working on yourself and others, you can quickly work through the layers of conditionings.

Some people doing the exercises may have deeper blockages connected to body sensations and feelings. Due to conditioning and painful experiences, they may have a deeper disconnect with their feelings. If this is the case for you, then you need be to more patient and take more time with your development.

It may be best to do these exercises when you are more peaceful and not under stress. If you are still having difficulties, then I would recommend our intuitive development program or private coaching.

If you are new to intuitive sensing, then you will need some patience and time to connect to your feelings. Some people have been conditioned due to their life experiences and sufferings to avoid connecting to their feelings.

Sadness

1. Find a recent experience "story" that triggered sadness.
2. Write down any sensations or feelings connected to this story.
3. Repeat this exercise three times and find differences in the experiences of sadness.
4. Write any key commonalities when you tune into "stories" of sadness.

Anger

1. Find a recent experience "story" that triggered anger.

2. Write down any body sensations or feelings connected to this "story."

3. Repeat this exercise three times and find differences in the experiences of anger.

4. Write any key commonalities when you tune into "stories" of anger.

Fear

1. Find a recent experience "story" that triggered fear.

2. Write down any body sensations or feelings connected to this "story."

3. Repeat this exercise three times and find differences in the experiences of fear.

4. Write any key commonalities when you tune into "stories" of fear.

Grief

1. Find a recent experience "story" that triggered grief.

2. Write down any body sensations or feelings connected to this "story."

3. Repeat this exercise three times and find differences in the experiences of grief.

4. Write any key commonalities when you tune into "stories" of grief.

Worry

1. Find a recent experience "story" that triggered worry.

2. Write down any body sensations or feelings connected to this "story."

3. Repeat this exercise three times and find differences in the experiences of worry.

4. Write any key commonalities when you tune into "stories" of worry.

Compare and Contrast Exercise

1. Compare and contrast the experiences between the five emotions.

2. Write down any key differences of the feelings.

Not Safe

1. Find a recent experience "story" that triggered not feeling safe.

2. Write down any body sensations or feelings connected to this "story."

3. Repeat this exercise three times and find differences in the experience of not feeling safe.

4. Write any key commonalities when you tune into "stories" of not feeling safe.

Not Loved

1. Find a recent experience "story" that triggered not feeling loved.

2. Write down any body sensations or feelings connected to this "story."

3. Repeat this exercise three times and find differences in the experience of not feeling loved.

4. Write any key commonalities when you tune into "stories" of not feeling loved.

Not in Control

1. Find a recent experience "story" that triggered not feeling in control.

2. Write down any body sensations or feelings connected to this "story."

3. Repeat this exercise three times and find differences in the experience of not feeling in control.

4. Write any key commonalities when you tune into "stories" of not feeling in control.

Not Trusting

1. Find a recent experience "story" that triggered not trusting.

2. Write down any body sensations or feelings connected to this "story."

3. Repeat this exercise three times and find differences in the experience of not trusting.

4. Write any key commonalities when you tune into "stories" of not trusting.

Compare and Contrast Exercise

1. Compare and contrast the experiences between the four issues.

2. Write down any key differences of the feelings.

Chapter 23

Applying "Who Am I?"

After working through the exercises with the nine layers, you will start to get an intuitive sense of the feelings connected to those experiences. You will be applying the "Who am I" (WAI) questions to the experiences of the previous chapter.

1. Who am I without this story?
2. Who am I if I let go of story?
3. Who am I if I am not this story?
4. Who am I if I can trust more to let go?

The reason you are doing it in this sequence is so that you get a sense of the "before" and "after" you apply the WAI questions. It is important to remember this is not about getting an immediate mental answer from the self-inquiry. The purpose is to communicate to the subconscious to evoke and bring to the surface what is unconscious and forgotten. You may bring up the emotions such as anger, fear, grief, and other sorrows and issues connected to safety, control, and trust. You will be asking the self-inquiring questions to either the heart and/or the gut in silence, as they are two major areas storing unconscious conditionings. Just feel for a response, whatever it may be. It may be pleasant or unpleasant. If you feel nothing, then just be patient and allow the subconscious time to process.

As you start to work through the surface layer, and then the medium and deeper layers over time, the deepest layer of the human psyche starts to reveal itself. As emotions and issues related safety, control, and trust are processed and resolved, the deeper sufferings related to your own life or to your parents, ancestors, the collective, or other existences will become conscious. Often times, the deepest layers are connected to your relationships to existence, the meaning of life, and divinity.

In the steps below, you will start applying WAI to the nine types of suffering.

Sadness

1. Ask WAI questions to the heart.
2. Write down what sensations you feel now about the "story" of sadness.
3. Ask WAI questions to the gut.
4. Write down what sensations you feel now about the "story" of sadness.

Anger

1. Ask WAI questions to the heart.
2. Write down what sensations you feel now about the "story" of anger.
3. Ask WAI questions to the gut.
4. Write down what sensations you feel now about the "story" of anger.

Fear

1. Ask WAI questions to the heart.
2. Write down what sensations you feel now about the "story" of fear.
3. Ask WAI questions to the gut.
4. Write down what sensations you feel now about the "story" of fear.

Grief

1. Ask WAI questions to the heart.
2. Write down what sensations you feel now about the "story" of grief.
3. Ask WAI questions to the gut.
4. Write down what sensations you feel now about the "story" of grief.

Worry

1. Ask WAI questions to the heart.

2. Write down what sensations you feel now about the "story" of worry.

3. Ask WAI questions to the gut.

4. Write down what sensations you feel now about the "story" of worry.

Not safe

1. Ask WAI questions to the heart.

2. Write down what sensations you feel now about the "story" of not feeling safe.

3. Ask WAI questions to the gut.

4. Write down what sensations you feel now about the "story" of not feeling safe.

Not loved

1. Ask WAI questions to the heart.

2. Write down what sensations you feel now about the "story" of not feeling loved.

3. Ask WAI questions to the gut.

4. Write down what sensations you feel now about the "story" of not feeling loved.

Not in control

1. Ask WAI questions to the heart.

2. Write down what sensations you feel now about the "story" of not feeling in control.

3. Ask WAI questions to the gut.

4. Write down what sensations you feel now about the "story" of not feeling in control.

Not trusting

1. Ask WAI questions to the heart.

2. Write down what sensations you feel now about the "story" of not trusting.

3. Ask WAI questions to the gut.

4. Write down what sensations you feel now about the "story" of not trusting.

Chapter 24

How to Work with Issues

In the previous chapters, you learned about the nine types of suffering. You also practiced getting a sense of what each type feels like in the exercises. Each issue can have energies related to one of these nine types and may have components of fear, anger, control, safety, etc. The HWP is simplified to work on subconscious conditioning held in the heart or gut, the region that contains most of the core human issues.

The chart below illustrates the general flow of the HWP. If you are working on yourself or others, you can start by rating the problem from zero to ten, with zero being no problem, peaceful, and ten being the worst, the most stressful. You start by asking your intuition to sense if the initial layer is in the heart or gut. You put your awareness in the heart or gut. Think about your problem or issue and get a sense for immediate body sensations such as heaviness, tightness, or tension in the heart or gut. Once you sense it, determine which of the nine types it is related to. Apply the WAI and notice the shift. Repeat this process until the stress rating goes down to zero.

Rate the issue from 0 to 10. 0-no problem, 10-most stressful

Physical or Non-physical Issues

HWP Process	Example
Is it in Heart or in Gut	Sadness in Heart
Apply WAI	WAI if I am let go of sadness
Next Layer: Heart or Gut	Fear
Apply WAI	Who am I if I let go of the stories about fear
Next Layer: Heart or Gut	Safety
Apply WAI	Who am I if I can trust more when I don't feel safe

Repeat the process until the rate goes to 0

Other Helpful Tips:

If your stress rating gets down to one or two but does not go all the way to zero, there are often several issues. The issues are often related to letting go of fear, safety, trust, and control. If these issues come up, then say to the heart or gut: "Who am I if I can trust the divine more?" The subconscious is directly connected to the greater universal intelligence. You must ask the greater divine force within you to help you release and let go.

If you are experiencing some difficulty applying these techniques, then it is best to have some customized training and coaching from a master practitioner and trainer to help you sense and develop your intuition. You have subconscious blocks preventing you from connecting to your feelings. I've noticed that some clients have disconnected or dissociated their body from feelings because of sufferings related to trauma, abuse, or painful experiences. Also, many people have been conditioned to avoid feelings due to criticism or shame for showing emotions and vulnerability. They have the perception that weakness will make them look bad and will threaten their survival.

Frequently Asked Questions

1. How do I heal chronic health issues or difficult life challenges relating to relationships, finances, or other areas?

If you have a difficult issue, it requires some time and patience to work through the layers. The conditionings of life are called "karmas" in the East. This means that behind your sufferings, you will have to work through them and process them through your heart to gain the insights or lessons of life. If not, the issues will remain, and you will likely repeat them until you learn. Usually, behind almost all issues and layers, the key lesson is love, spiritual growth, and awakening. This work is a dynamic letting go and releasing process – and often brings up a lot of suppressed conditioning that has become unconscious over the years. A key component of this healing is to turn stuck energies from a static state into dynamic state so they can be released. Much of our sorrows are held together by grief. With this process, the heart turns grief into a dynamic state commonly known as sadness. When sadness comes through, it is often a good sign that you are letting go and healing deeper unconscious layers. Often times, we must release the sorrows and grief of our parents and ancestors that have been held for many generations.

It is not realistic to expect complete healing or a turnaround of major life challenges in one or two sessions. That is why we ask clients to work with us over a three- to six-month period. During this time, we work to help them gain "insights." *When that happens, significant improvements can occur.* Also, the program is aimed at rebuilding the energetic foundations to process unconscious conditioning through your heart. It is also about retraining your neurology to automatically process the energies that are causing suffering. This program is intended to benefit you for the rest of your life. Hence, it cannot be done in one day. It must be done over time.

This work requires some patience because we are dealing with much unconscious conditioning that has been stored for many years – and we must allow it to bubble up as layers of the onion before it can be peeled off. Some people experience significant shifts, and some people tell us about miracles –but that should not be your expectation.

2. Can we use this process for children, family members, or friends?

Young children: When we get inquiries about helping children, no matter what age they are, and especially for young children, we recommend that people asking for help do a few sessions for themselves first. The children are the product of the DNA of both parents. They will feel everything the parents are going through psychically and empathically. DNA is like invisible antennae.

Whenever parents are stressed, worried, fearful, or experiencing other life issues, children will feel the same and will likely experience anxiety issues. In today's world, most parents are not trained in holistic means to address the energies behind their stressors. They actually have been conditioned to cope with them through distractions such as alcohol, smoking, food, shopping, etc. If these are the default ways of coping, then children will adopt them unconsciously.

As for the children of divorced parents, they are most likely to be struggling. In most cases, there is much resentment and bitterness toward each party. Children will feel parts of themselves energetically at war with each other, which will cause lots of confusion, anxiety, or other behavioral issues. If parents are holding negative thoughts (vibrations), even if not verbalized, their children will absorb the negativity.

The focus of our sessions is to help parents come to peace through releasing the energetics behind the wounds. If the wounds fully heal and the grievances are forgiven, then each parent can hold a space of love, acceptance, and positive thoughts toward the other.

Adult children, parent, spouse, other: The best way to help your loved one is to work through your own worries and fears. Work through your triggers relating to the situation and come to a deep acceptance and peace for the situation and the person. When you get to a space of not needing to fix or "save" anyone, then your loved ones will most likely come to you for advice and healing.

Many people report the techniques work for themselves, friends, or clients – but are not working on family as effectively. Trying to help loved ones can be the most difficult, because there are so many attachments, as opposed to helping someone who is not as close.

Whenever we get requests for healing a family member, I usually recommend that the person asking do some sessions on themselves first. After doing so, that person shifts and often reports that the family member has changed as well – even though we never worked on the family member with the issue. What happens is that the person shifts and his/her vibrations change– and then the family member shifts as well.

3. What does the HWP group or individual session experience actually feel like?

During the session, most clients experience releasing in many ways – sometimes through tears, physical sensations such as pain, vibrations, yawning, energy movements, etc. Also, unconscious conditioning in the form of forgotten memories and feelings are likely to arise.

As the conditioning comes to the surface, it may be very uncomfortable. Sometimes people may feel nauseous, heaviness, difficulty breathing, sharp pain, and other sensations. When such sensations come up, it is best to stay present and allow the practitioner to guide you through them.

As unconscious conditioning surfaces, you are likely going to become conscious of issues related to safety, control, and approval (not being loved). When there is a letting go of these issues, you will likely experience some sadness and then relief, and then the process repeats itself.

After multiple layers get worked through, key life insights can come in one or more sessions. Small insights build up to larger insights for a much better picture of yourself, and then your divine plan becomes revealed on this journey.

4. Can you explain why we can still get triggered after working on an issue?

Sometimes we are still triggered even after we have worked on an issue. To better understand why this happens, let's look at the issue through the metaphor of taking out the trash. In the trash can, there are three layers of trash: the surface, the middle, and the deepest. Because there is so much trash in the subconscious, we are simply not aware of the deepest layer when the surface and medium layers are processed. That's why you may be still triggered after working on the issue.

Often times, the very raw emotions of your childhood self and your relationships to safety and love are the deeper issues. Other deep issues are your relationships to the meaning of life, existence, and divinity.

For those with lifelong issues like chronic health, depression, or other long-term problems, you must be willing to go the full length of the marathon and work through the deepest layers. With the most difficult issues, this may take time, and it can be months and sometimes a few years to turn things around. As I mentioned with my chronic conditions, it took years for different areas to improve.

5. How do I measure my progress?

A good measurement of improvement is to see how long it takes to get over an issue that has affected you. In the past, a trigger may have taken weeks to get over. If you see that it only takes a few days to get over an issue, then that's a significant improvement. As more time passes, the few days to get over something turns into a few hours. That's how I have seen my own progress. The same issues take less and less time to process and get over.

6. What are the difficulties and challenges of the HWP journey?

For those doing the HWP, you will need to understand that the program is not about learning short-term techniques but is designed to give you long-term development to bring your happiness and inner peace to your life for years to come. Although some techniques can be applied to give you quick stress and pain relief, you must understand that the methodologies and processes are used to dig deep into your subconscious to release suffering there.

The first three to six months are likely to be the most challenging and uncomfortable because practitioners are likely to experience significant detoxing and releasing, both physically and emotionally. You may become very emotional as you connect to forgotten memories to release very old emotions related to grief, sadness, anger, and other sorrows.

Your physical self may also reorient during this period because, as subconscious energies get released, they will push on physical organs and structures. You may feel pain and discomfort from this release. If this happens, you are likely to experience more insecurities such as fears and worries. That's why we encourage participants to work with us directly either through group or individual work over a six-month period to deal with changes. This is like a hand-holding period.

Of course, you can do this work on your own, but if you don't have experience, it may be challenging. You may have heard of the term "healing crisis." This happens when unconscious issues come up, and it can be frightening because of the lack of guidance. You might feel lost, have unexplainable physical discomforts or symptoms, or undergo what others have described as the "dark night of the soul." If you have the support of an experienced guide, then the different phases of growth can be worked through with minimal drama.

You are likely to experience a lot of physical and emotional ups and downs on this journey. The HWP reorients and teaches you to be present with your feelings instead of avoiding them. It trains you to get to the energies behind your thoughts and stories. Your connections and sensitivities to feelings will be heightened.

Growth and personal change will likely be a double-edged sword though. As you become more connected to feelings and process your conditioning with the heart, you will feel the deeper inner peace, stillness, silence, bliss, and other positive attributes of infinity in your heart. However, as you work through your subconscious conditioning, you will also feel and become aware of what is deeply hidden in the subconscious. Being more connected is like having a bigger flashlight – the more light you have, the more you can see in the darkness – and you will notice that there are deeper issues you were previously unconscious of.

7. What is the HWP focused on developing?

During the initial six months, the HWP is focused on "unconditioning your conditioning." In ancient times, intuitive feelings were much valued because we were actually intimately connected to nature and its creations. Our intuitive feelings represent whether we are living in harmony or against nature. There are two problems of modern society: (1) People are conditioned to process their life experiences with the mind. When the sufferings of life are not properly processed, they go into subconscious. (2) Conditioning makes people avoid being vulnerable and experiencing pain. Hence, the vast majority of people are not connected intimately to the intuitive feelings of the heart due to pain and suffering.

In the initial development period of the HWP, people are learning to feel and become sensitive to their feelings. This period is about learning to become intimately aware of your intuitive feelings. In order to do this, you must let go of your conditioning and your fears of avoiding pain and suffering. As you do the work during this period, you will learn to process these feelings through the heart. Although it is difficult, the mind and ego will start to relearn that it is safe and ok to process those uncomfortable feelings. Over time, you will start to live and become a more fully sensitive being instead of constantly avoiding bad feelings. When you release the energies behind bad feelings through the heart, they will no longer be lying dormant in the subconscious.

For those interested in specifically improving their intuition, you must work through the suffering and the programming in the subconscious. There are numerous reasons why people are blocked from intuition. You might have avoided processing these feelings due to your programming and to put forth a strong personal image.

You may have had experiences of being disapproved, criticized, or ridiculed by others when you shared your intuition, feelings, and experiences with unexplainable phenomena. Your intuition and feelings may have been dismissed because they were not based on logic and analysis. You may have been disconnected from the universal intelligence or the invisible divine force that holds life together.

You must let go of fear, fully connecting to your feelings and becoming vulnerable to them. With HWP, you can work through all these experiences to improve your intuition.

8. What is the difference between the HWP and Chinese Energetics?

The Heart Wisdom Process is focused on working deeply with the subconscious. Chinese Energetics courses and training offer some of the best techniques for relieving pain and stress quickly. Chinese Energetics techniques effectively resolve negative patterns and relieve suffering for medium-to-surface layer issues.

However, if the deeper subconscious causes are not processed, then the problem can either come back or manifest in a different form. Here are some examples. You can fix a symptom like a knee pain in minutes, but you might not have gotten to the cause, and other pains will manifest in different forms. You can relieve stress quickly, but if you don't get to the root, you may end up re-experiencing the same types of situations or relationships that cause stress over and over again.

When you resolve the subconscious patterns, then you simply don't attract those situations or people into your life anymore.

9. Why it is important to commit to the HWP long-term?

- It takes time to learn to work with the subconscious and cannot be done in just a few sessions.
- It will take time to process and let go of decades of programming.
- Not regularly working on the process can lead to a healing crisis and premature understanding and conclusions.
- The deepest conditioning can be released when the ego is ready.

10. Can you tell me more about Amma, ashrams, and India?

This work has been developed while spending time in the presence of spiritual masters, modern-day living saints. When you are in their presence, you are exposed to high amounts of spirit energies that act as catalysts for personal and spiritual growth. The energies purify you by bringing the unconscious to the conscious. When this happens, you have an opportunity to learn the lessons of life at an accelerated pace. If you do, then old patterns or karmas can break and you don't have to relive your repeated sufferings over and over again.

My recommendation is to initially start by visiting them and receiving darshan during the regular US/European tour. You can ask for a blessing on whatever aspect of life you need help with, whether for health, wealth, relationships, or happiness. You might experience discomfort and not fun experiences as your patterns break and release.

If your interest deepens, I would encourage you to spend more time and possibly volunteer at programs and retreats. Eventually, you may have the desire to visit ashrams and spend more time there.

You can find further information at the following websites:

- Hugging Amma, www.amma.org
- Amma Karunamayi, www.karunamayi.org
- Mother Meera, www.mothermeera.org
- Ramana Maharishi, www.sriramanamaharshi.org

11. How do I contact you?

www.heartwisdomprocess.com

Dear Cousin Karen!
Wishing our family a happy
drama free life.
Have a great rest of 2017!
Blessings!! :)

10/24/17

Made in the USA
Lexington, KY
04 August 2017